Table of Contents

Introduction

The region of Northeast Asia is the fastest growing part of the global economy, produces upwards of one-fifth of the world's economic output, and consists of nearly nineteen percent of the world's trade. Likewise, Asia contains five of twenty of the world's largest economies and four of ten of the world's largest militaries.[1] Stability in the region benefits South Korean growth and prosperity, U.S. national interests, and the global economy.[2]

The United States has had a significant military presence in the Republic of Korea (ROK) since World War II in order to assist the ROK in preserving a democratic form of government and preventing the violent reunification of North and South Korea into a state that favors communist ideology. Initially, the U.S. military aided in South Korea's recovery from Japanese occupation, but this role shifted during the Korean War from 1950-1953, with the U.S. military operating under the auspices of a United Nations (UN) resolution. More than twenty nations provided military support to United Nations operations in South Korea during that period, and while many of these countries have benefited from the preservation of South Korea's sovereignty, the United States has borne the majority of the military burden in Korea since the armistice of 1953. The deterioration of the economic situation in the United States, compounded by the duration of the wars in Afghanistan and Iraq, has put excessive burdens on the U.S. military and the United States. In stark contrast, the growth of the ROK Army has not kept pace with the continuing growth of the South Korean economy. Instead, the rising expense of security on the Korean Peninsula has increasingly fallen to the American taxpayer.

---

[1] *The Economist Pocket World in Figures, 2011 Edition* (London, England: Penguin Group: Hamish Hamilton Ltd. in association with The Economist Newspaper Ltd., 2011).

[2] Carl (U.S. Senator) Levin, "Hearing to Receive Testimony on U.S. Pacific Command and U.S. Forces Korea in Review of the Defense Authorization Request for Fiscal Year 2012 and the Future Years Defense Program," (2011).

Force reduction on the Korean Peninsula has been a topic for political debate since 1953.[3] The policies that have evolved since then and current regional security agreements provide an explanation for the current U.S. military posture. What does not explain the current military posture is the relative improvement in the South Korean economy as compared to the recent contraction of many national economies, including that of the U.S. If these economic trends continue as expected, the U.S. will be unable to sustain the current policies, strategies, and cooperative arrangements for securing the Korean Peninsula without added assistance from their South Korean and United Nations allies. Transferring the majority of the security burden onto the Republic of Korea will not erode the security situation between North and South Korea, but it will help focus U.S. Department of Defense budget cuts while allowing the U.S. military to implement more innovative solutions with a reduced force structure to achieve the same strategic end.

Analyzing the security and economic situations facing both countries, this monograph seeks to address the need for an alternative strategy for U.S. forces in the ROK in order to find ways and means that consider the mounting costs and strain on the operational force while maintaining the same strategic ends. That is, seeking more cost effective means to maintain the U.S./ROK alliance while continuing to deter North Korean aggression and maintain broader security objectives in the region.

This analysis begins by examining an evolving U.S. policy and strategy vis-à-vis Korea from an ends, ways, and means perspective in order to compare and contrast past assumptions to the current situation. This policy examination includes the history of the Korean Peninsula since the end of World War II as a means to explain the significance of South Korea to American

---

[3] Tae-Hwan Kwak, Wayne Pattersen, and Edward A. Olsen, *The Two Koreas in World Politics*, IFES research series (Seoul, Korea: Institute for Far Eastern Studies, Kyungnam University, 1983), 332-41.

regional objectives and interests, and explains how U.S./ROK relations fit into the broader national security strategy and why relations should continue in the future.

The monograph then looks toward the future and explores possible changes in the future security situation, changes brought about by the potential of a North Korean regime collapse and/or reunification of the two Koreas, in order to assess the resulting impacts on the U.S.-ROK relationship. These scenarios will be discussed based on current policy and strategy and will identify the likely expectations of the U.S. in relation to military and financial support. The U.S. is likely to bear much of the cost associated with reunification efforts if U.S. forces remain on the peninsula in significant numbers. This exploration should demonstrate the expanding financial burden to the American taxpayer and justify the pursuit of an alternative to the current strategy while emphasizing the Republic of Korea's ability and necessity to replace or replicate the gap currently filled by U.S. forces.

Finally, the monograph analyzes the risks and benefits associated with two alternatives for maintaining the security of South Korea in the years ahead. First, the study weighs the costs of continuing the security arrangement as it currently exists, in terms of both regional security and the economic security of the United States. The study then analyzes a proposed alternative strategy: shifting the majority of the security burden to the Republic of Korea.

This proposed alternative includes a reduction in U.S. combat forces (ground, sea, and air) offset by an increase in the number of forces used in an advisory role. As such, this new strategy proposal does not completely negate the necessity for some U.S. military personnel in the ROK, but rather, shifts the burden for tactical combat forces to the ROK while providing U.S. support in the form of advisors and operational level support forces. The monograph addresses the pros and cons of this alternative, examining its effectiveness in achieving security objectives, alleviating U.S. budget pressures, and revitalizing the U.S. military. It will also discuss the need to bolster ROK military capacity in order to replace the capabilities of U.S. forces, an area that the South Korean government will have to address. Potential ways in which the U.S. and ROK

3

can bolster this capacity includes U.S. foreign military sales, increased combined training, and increased participation in global United Nations missions.

Strategic Context

U.S military interests within the Republic of Korea are best understood within the strategic context in which forces are employed within the region. Army Doctrine Publication (ADP) 3-0 *Unified Land Operations* states, "Army forces are employed within a strategic context defined by the specific operational environment, the character of the friendly force, and the character of the threat. Underpinning the strategic context enables Army forces to preserve vital national interests."[4] The White House and U.S. Defense Department's January 2012 *Priorities for 21st Century Defense*, which provided strategic guidance for military planners, re-emphasized and re-focused U.S. economic and security interests towards the Western Pacific and East Asia including the Korean Peninsula.[5] However, the evolving strategic context requires an adaptive military solution that can still preserve vital national interests in the region while accounting for a deteriorating U.S. economy and a waning military force. An examination of the operational environment, character of the threat, and character of the friendly force reveals the conditions for U.S. force reduction in Korea that protects the enduring vital national interests in the region while realistically accounting for the fiscal constraints imposed by the current global economic situation.

ADP 3-0 defines the operational environment as "a composite of conditions, circumstances, and influences that effect the employment of capabilities and bear on the decisions of the commander."[6] Analyzing the operational environment includes the analysis of operational

---

[4] Department of the Army, *ADP 3-0 Unified Land Operations* (Washington, DC: Department of the Army, 2011), 2.

[5] Department of Defense, "Sustaining U.S. Global Leadership: Priorities for 21st Century Defense." (Washington, DC: Department of Defense, 2012), 2.

[6] Headquarters, *ADP 3-0 Unified Land Operations*, 2.

4

variables such as political, military, economic, and social circumstances.[7] Although these are not the only variables that must be analyzed, they are the most germane to this strategic context. These particular operational variables describe the background and history of the Korean Peninsula and set the stage for use of U.S. forces to preserve vital interests that have been determined over time and set the conditions, circumstances, and influences for U.S. military presence. In essence, the background of the division of Korea and U.S. involvement helps to define the operational environment.

The character of the threat is a vital component to the trinity of strategic context. The threat instigates the necessity for military force when diplomatic efforts fail to reach a policy end state, or as famously noted by war theorist Carl von Clausewitz, war is an extension of policy where the object is to compel the enemy to one's will.[8] The North Korean war machine has aimed to achieve the ends of unifying the two Koreas under a Communist government by force, if necessary, while maintaining the survival of the regime.[9] Their primary means of achieving this end has been through building a robust conventional fighting force capable of dominating the peninsula by ways of a military-centric political base.[10] The Korean People's Army has also built an asymmetric capability to offset the more technologically advanced equipment of the United

---

[7] Ibid, 2.

[8] Carl von Clausewitz, *On War,* ed. and trans. by Michael Howard and Peter Paret (Princeton, N.J.: Princeton University Press, 1984), 610.

[9] Jennifer Peloso, *The Two Koreas*, The Reference Shelf (New York: H.W. Wilson, 2004), 10-12.

[10] Walter L. Sharp, "Statement of General Walter L. Sharp Commander, United Nations Command; Commander, United States-Republic of Korea Combined Forces Command; and Commander, United States Forces Korea Before the House Armed Services Committee, April 6, 2011," 6-12.

States and South Korea.[11] Since early 2001, their means shifted to a nuclear capability that could

thwart U.S. nuclear capabilities while remaining determined of their policy ends.[12]

Based on the operational environment, U.S. Army forces are employed to adequately

deter or defeat an enemy threat. The character of the friendly force determines the proper

composition and disposition to counter enemy threats. ADP 3-0 describes the character of the

friendly force as part of a larger effort known as unified action.[13] Leaders that can collaborate

with entities beyond their control and understand, influence, and cooperate with unified action

partners to effectively operate as part of a larger national effort are required to lead the Army

force.[14] In the context of military efforts in Korea, the friendly force is composed of a

multinational military force primarily with forces from South Korea and the United States. To

achieve their strategic ends, the U.S. and ROK must unify their ways and means. Both countries

aim to achieve a stable environment in order to allow for economic growth and prosperity.

Stability on the peninsula allows South Korea to expand financially while contributing to Asian

and global markets, a benefit to the United States. However, South Korea has the additional

strategic goal of reunifying the two Koreas under one democratic government. The United States,

on the other hand, prefers to maintain the status quo of a divided peninsula in order to alleviate

any further economic burdens, according to some South Korean scholars.[15] The ways and means

of maintaining stability in the region focus on a strong ground force supplemented by technically

---

[11] Anthony H. Cordesman and Andrew Gagel, *The Korean Military Balance: Comparative Korean Forces and the Forces of Key Neighboring States: Main Report* (Washington, DC: Center for Strategic and International Studies, 2011), xiii.

[12] Charles L. Pritchard, *Failed Diplomacy: The Tragic Story of How North Korea Got the Bomb* (Washington, DC: Brookings Institution Press, 2007), 1, 150-53.

[13] Department of the Army, *ADP 3-0 Unified Land Operations*, 3.

[14] Ibid, 3.

[15] Tae-Hwan Kwak, *U.S.-Korean Relations, 1882-1982*, IFES research series (Seoul, Korea: Kyungnam University Press, 1982), 66.

superior naval and air forces. The disparity between U.S. and ROK military contributions to the ways and means accounts for the bifurcated characterization of the friendly force.

The Operational Environment

The Korean Peninsula lays in the heart of Northeast Asia with a landmass twice the size of the American state of Indiana. China borders Korea to the north with the Yellow Sea and China to their west. To the south and east lies the East Sea and Japan. Korea has experienced war, occupation, and conflict seemingly since its inception. Currently, the peninsula is separated along the 38th parallel into two countries, the communist Democratic People's Republic of Korea (DPRK) to the north and the democratic Republic of Korea (ROK) in the south. The history of the two Koreas before and after World War II provides the circumstances that led to the Korean War between the DPRK and the ROK, with participation by China and the United States. Examining this history aids in understanding the policies and military representation on the Korean Peninsula up to the present day, assists in the prediction of future policies and security arrangements in the region, which allows for the proposal of alternatives. Despite the current strength of the diplomatic and military alliance between South Korea and the United States, attempts to withdraw American troops from the ROK by previous administrations have been tried and failed to some degree since the end of the conflict in July 1953. The current U.S. policy towards the ROK and military posture in their country reflects these past attempts and gives basis for a discussion to draw down U.S. troop presence in Korea or maintain the status quo.

Pre-World War II

The Korean Peninsula has been of interest for her neighbors for many centuries. China, Russia, and Japan found Korea's harbors to be of great value and used them as embarkation and debarkation points to wage war on each other.[16] Korea was dominated by China from at least the seventh century until the closing of the nineteenth century (BCE), adopting Chinese culture, language, and ideology.[17] In the 13th century, Kublai Khan launched two invasions on Japan from Korea.[18] However, Japan's power increased significantly during the Edo Period (1615-1868) and began to rival its neighbors by the middle of the nineteenth century. In 1876, the Japanese established a "most favored nation" status with Korea in the Treaty of Kangwha, which ultimately contributed to the Sino-Japanese war in 1894 and led to Korea's annexation and brutal occupation by the Japanese empire.[19] The basis for the formal annexation in 1910 was an agreement between U.S. Secretary of War, William Howard Taft, and the Japanese foreign minister regarding Japan's unhindered domination of the Korean Peninsula in exchange for the United States' unimpeded domination of the Philippines by the Japanese.[20] Japanese domination spread into China and other parts of Asia and eventually resulted in World War II and competition with major world powers. The Cairo Conference of 1943 between the United States, Great Britain, and China resulted in an alliance to defeat Japan, return all occupied Chinese territory back to China, and a declaration that Korea would be free and independent.[21] However, the Yalta Conference between the United States, Great Britain, and the Soviet Union held in February 1945 outlined the division of territory between the allies in post war Europe, as well as the Soviet Union's agreement to enter the war against Japan after the defeat of Germany.[22] In

---

[16] James F. Schnabel, *Policy and Direction: The First Year*, United States Army in the Korean War, v. 3. (Washington, DC: Office of the Chief of Military History, United States Army, 1972), 2.

[17] Ibid, 2.

[18] Ibid, 2.

[19] John S. Bowman, ed., *Columbia Chronologies of Asian History and Culture* (New York: Columbia University Press, 2000), 141-49.

[20]Don Oberdorfer, *The Two Koreas: A Contemporary History*, New ed. (New York: Basic Books, 2001), 5.

[21] Kwak, *U.S.-Korean Relations, 1882-1982*: 65-67.

[22] Ibid., 253.

early August of 1945 after the Allies declared victory in Europe and victory in Japan was imminent, the Allied heads of state held the Potsdam Conference that reconfirmed the terms outlined in the Cairo Conference.[23] While endorsing the terms of the Potsdam Conference, the Soviet's declaration of war on Japan placed great pressure on the United States for serious consideration to policy regarding the future of the Korean Peninsula. According to Korea scholar Don Oberdorfer, "[s]uddenly Washington realized that Russian occupation of Korea would have important military implications for the future of Japan and East Asia."[24]

Post-World War II

During the eve of Japan's surrender with Soviet forces moving towards the Korean Peninsula, two U.S. Army Lieutenant Colonels designated areas of responsibility for Soviet, Chinese, and U.S. forces. Neither officer—Dean Rusk, who would later become Secretary of State, and Charles Bonesteel, who would later be commander of U.S. Forces-Korea (USFK)— had any expertise regarding Korea nor did they consult with any Korea experts. They made the decision to divide the peninsula virtually at the halfway point along the thirty-eighth parallel based on visually proportioned division of a *National Geographic* map.[25] The Soviets agreed with this designation and moved forces all the way to the separation line. In November 1947, the United Nations adopted a resolution proposed by the United States that would unify Korean government through free elections under UN supervision, however, the Soviet Union greatly rejected this proposal and the establishment of separate governments was established in Korea.[26] As the birth of the cold war emerged, the two areas of responsibility became the U.S.-supported

---

[23] Chae-Jin Lee, *A Troubled Peace: U.S. Policy and the Two Koreas* (Baltimore: Johns Hopkins University Press, 2006), 18-19.

[24] Oberdorfer, *The Two Koreas: A Contemporary History*: 5-6.

[25] Ibid., 6.

[26] Chang-Il Ohn, "The Joint Chiefs of Staff and U.S. Policy and Strategy Regarding Korea, 1945-1953" (University of Kansas, 1983), 64.

Republic of Korea on August 15, 1948 and the Soviet-supported Democratic People's Republic of Korea on September 9, 1948 and have been further designated, albeit unofficially, as North Korea and South Korea.[27] Arguably, tension between the United States and Soviet Union was the cause of the Korean division, not the effect.[28]

The Truman Doctrine laid much of the foundation for the presence of U.S. forces in post-World War II South Korea.[29] The origins of the Truman Doctrine, which also set the stage for the Cold War, came from a speech given by President Truman before a joint session of the U.S. Congress on March 12, 1947.[30] The purpose of the speech was to convince Congress to allow foreign aid to Greece and Turkey in their quest to resist communist influence. The cornerstone of Truman's speech that gave birth to his doctrine stated,

> At present moment in world history nearly every nation must choose between alternative ways of life. The choice is too often not a free one. One way of life is based upon the will of the majority, and is distinguished by free institutions, representative government, free elections, guaranties of individual liberty, freedom of speech and religion, and freedom from political oppression. The second way of life is based upon the will of a minority forcibly imposed upon the majority. It relies upon terror and oppression, a controlled press and radio, fixed elections, and the suppression of personal freedoms. I believe that it must be the policy of the United States to support free peoples who are resisting attempted subjugation by armed minorities or by outside pressures. I believe that we must assist free peoples to work out their own destinies in their own way.[31]

---

[27] Oberdorfer, *The Two Koreas: A Contemporary History*: 7.

[28] Edward A. Olsen, *U.S. Policy and the Two Koreas* (San Francisco: World Affairs Council of Northern California, 1988), 2.

[29] Robert J. Pauly, *The Ashgate Research Companion to US Foreign Policy* (Farnham, England; Burlington, Vt.: Ashgate, 2010), 31.

[30] Heiko Meiertöns, *The Doctrines of US Security Policy: An Evaluation under International Law* (Cambridge: Cambridge University Press, 2010), 100-01.

[31] Harry S. Truman, "Recommendation for Assistance to Greece and Turkey: Address of The President of the United States," ed. U.S. House of Representatives (Washington, DC, 1947).

Truman's doctrine gave little guidance as to which geographical regions were of strategic value to the United States; however, it seemingly provided carte blanche to strategists and military planners for basing U.S. forces in Korea and around the world.[32]

The Korean War

Soviet-trained Kim Il-sung, who fought as a guerilla fighter against the Japanese in China during World War II, led North Korea. Kim had close ties with Soviet leader Joseph Stalin and sought his approval and assistance to invade South Korea to reunite the two Koreas under a communist banner.[33] South Korea was led by Syngman Rhee who lived in exile during most of the Japanese occupation of Korea.[34] Kim Il-sung had strong contempt for Syngman Rhee believing that he was a puppet leader under the purview of the imperialist United States.[35] Despite Stalin's refusal of Kim's requests for support, the North Korean leader prepared his army to invade south of the 38th parallel. Saber rattling and cross-border clashes led South Korean and U.S. military officials to believe that an invasion from the north was imminent. The timing of it, however, was undetermined.[36] By June 1950, Soviet forces had pulled out of North Korea and U.S. forces had moved back to Japan to focus on Japan's reconstruction. Only a 600-man contingent of officers and men from the Korean Military Advisory Group (KMAG) remained in South Korea to advise and train the ROK army.[37] On June 25, 1950, seven divisions and two armored brigades of the North Korean People's Army (KPA) invaded across the 38th parallel with

---

[32] Walter A. McDougall, *Promised Land, Crusader State: The American Encounter with the World Since 1776* (Boston: Houghton Mifflin, 1997), 164.

[33] Oberdorfer, *The Two Koreas: A Contemporary History*: 8-9.

[34] Ibid, 8-9.

[35] Ibid, 8-9.

[36] Allan Reed Millett, *The War for Korea, 1950-1951: They Came From the North*, Modern War Studies (Lawrence: University Press of Kansas, 2010), 25.

[37] Ibid., 12.

the intent to destroy the ROK army, oust President Rhee, and reunify the two Koreas under a communist government.[38] That same day, the United Nations Security Council censured DPRK's invasion of the ROK with United Nations Security Council Resolution 82. Two days later, United Nations Security Council Resolution 83 recommended member nations to provide military assistance to the ROK. For 1,128 days, sixteen UN member states led by the U.S. fought and repelled a Chinese and Soviet backed KPA from the forceful reunification of the two Koreas. Ultimately, the Korean War set the conditions and circumstances for future U.S. foreign policy in South Korea.[39]

By summer 1951, both UN forces and the Chinese backed KPA had gained and lost territory north and south of the 38th parallel. A stalemate ensued in June 1951 with the primary belligerents back on their respective sides of the original border at the 38th parallel while armistice negotiations commenced. As the United States focused on security in Europe and rebuilding Japan, the policy was to restore the pre-conflict border at the 38th parallel while keeping communism out of South Korea in order to create a buffer between the Soviet Union's expansion into Asia and U.S. rebuilding efforts in Japan.[40] Although the U.S. had every reason to end hostilities in Korea, the South Korean government wanted no part in armistice negotiations, vying for reunification of the two Koreas by force, if necessary.[41] Likewise, the U.S. gave credence to the Truman Doctrine, believing that weaker countries of the world would fall to communism if it were not stifled in Korea.[42] China and the Soviet Union had every intention to

---

[38] Ibid, 12.

[39] Bureau of East Asian and Pacific Affairs and U.S. Department of State, "South Korea," U.S. Department of State, http://www.state.gov/r/pa/ei/bgn/2800.htm (accessed October 8, 2011).

[40] Millett, *The War for Korea, 1950-1951: They Came From the North*: 13-14.

[41] Bureau of East Asian and Pacific Affairs and U.S. Department of State, "South Korea," U.S. Department of State, http://www.state.gov/r/pa/ei/bgn/2800.htm (accessed October 8, 2011).

[42] Ohn, "The Joint Chiefs of Staff and U.S. Policy and Strategy Regarding Korea, 1945-1953," 208.

delay armistice negotiations.[43] This benefited the Soviet Union by distracting the United States from their efforts in Europe while committing troops and resources to far-off Korea.[44] China also benefited by being able to train their armed forces against a western superpower while they gained power for defeating UN forces in many battles. They had earned dominance in the armistice negotiations and relished in their budding prospects of becoming a world power.[45] The Korean War ended on July 27, 1953 with over 36,000 American service members killed and nearly 100,000 more wounded. Ostensibly, the United States gained little, if anything, for their participation in the Korean War. Conditions on the peninsula were more suitable to the U.S. prior to June 1950. However, the war allowed the United States to demonstrate their assertion that they would not allow communism to spread to free states and would remain committed to supporting those nations who wished to remain free from communism. Despite the Cold War's end in the early 1990s, a sizeable American military force remains in South Korea annually consuming millions of U.S. tax dollars in order to deter continued communist aggression by North Korea towards the Republic of Korea.

Post-Korean War Policies

In the wake of the 1953 armistice, the ROK and U.S. governments solidified their alliance with the Mutual Defense Treaty of 1953 signed in Washington on October 1 of that year. Since the parties signed the treaty, it has remained in effect without amendments or alterations. Article three of the treaty states,

> Each Party recognizes that an armed attack in the Pacific area on either of the Parties in territories now under their respective control, or hereafter recognized by one of the Parties as lawfully brought under the administrative control of the other, would be dangerous to its own peace and

---

[43] Millett, *The War for Korea, 1950-1951: They Came From the North*: 14.

[44] Ibid, 14.

[45] Ibid, 14.

13

safety and declares that it would act to meet the common danger in accordance with its constitutional processes.[46]

Although the verbiage within the treaty does not clearly state a requirement for the U.S. military to maintain a presence within the ROK, commanders and politicians who advocate a troop presence have referenced the Mutual Defense Treaty as a writ to justify troop strength and expenditures in South Korea as the only method to deter North Korean aggression. Former USFK and United Nations Command commander, General Walter Sharp, asserted in testimony to the U.S. Congress in April 2011 that, "U.S. force presence in Korea is [also] a vital part of maintaining security commitments to the ROK established under the Mutual Defense Treaty."[47] The ROK government has been apprehensive of Washington's commitment to maintain U.S. troops in their country, fearing the United States might abandon them in a time of need, despite the U.S. military's desire to maintain a formidable presence in Korea. Some of this apprehension comes from the verbiage in article three of the treaty and the reference to each country's commitment of forces under constitutional processes.[48] A signing statement at the end of the treaty further exacerbated ROK fears of U.S. abandonment. The statement is the understanding of the United States of America:

> It is the understanding of the United States that neither party is obligated, under Article 3 of the above Treaty, to come to the aid of the other except in case of an external armed attack against such party; nor shall anything in the present Treaty be construed as requiring the United States to give assistance to Korea except in the event of an armed attack against territory which has

---

[46] United States and Republic of Korea, *Mutual Defense Treaty Between the United States of America and the Republic of Korea, Signed at Washington October 1, 1953* (Washington, DC: GPO, 1953).

[47] Sharp, "Statement of General Walter L. Sharp Commander, United Nations Command; Commander, United States-Republic of Korea Combined Forces Command; and Commander, United States Forces Korea Before the House Armed Services Committee, April 6, 2011," 3.

[48] William E. Berry and Army War College (U.S.) Strategic Studies Institute., *The Invitation to Struggle: Executive and Legislative Competition Over the U.S. Military Presence on the Korean Peninsula* (Carlisle Barracks, PA.: Strategic Studies Institute, U.S. Army War College, 1996), 2-3.

been recognized by the United States or lawfully brought under the administrative control of the Republic of Korea.[49]

Although the treaty does not legally bind the U.S. to maintain a military presence in the ROK, it has been a source of justification to maintain a presence for both governments.[50] By the time the treaty was signed in 1953, the United Nations Command, under the purview of an American commander, had 20 ROK Army divisions and two U.S. divisions supplemented by American air and sea power in defense of South Korea.[51] Policy makers from both countries have attempted to downsize these numbers as much as they have tried to justify them.

The devastation of war left the Korean Peninsula in shambles, but a negotiated reprieve from combat operations allowed both sides to focus on rebuilding.[52] The justification to maintain troop strengths and a military presence in Korea stems from the recognition by policy makers of Korea's strategically advanced placement with regards to Communist China, Soviet Union/Russian Federation, and North Korea and the post-war rebuilding efforts in Japan. This point is best illustrated by Korea scholar, Tae-hwan Kwak, "[s]ince 1950 U.S. policy makers have recognized the importance of the geostrategic location of Korea in the event of limited war and they have also recognized that a Communist Korea could pose a grave threat to U.S. security/core interests in Japan and the Western Pacific."[53] The policy to maintain U.S. forces in Korea built and maintained a stable environment while allowing the ROK to focus on building their military, infrastructure, and economy.

---

[49] United States and Republic of Korea, *Mutual Defense Treaty Between the United States of America and the Republic of Korea, Signed at Washington October 1, 1953* (Washington, DC: GPO, 1953).

[50] Claude Albert Buss, *The United States and the Republic of Korea: Background for Policy*, Hoover International Studies (Stanford, Calif.: Hoover Institution Press, Stanford University, 1982), 57.

[51] Millett, *The War for Korea, 1950-1951: They Came From the North*: 15.

[52] Kelvin C. Marshment, "The U.S. Ground Combat Experience in Korea: In Defense of U.S. Interests or a Strategic Dinosaur" (Command and General Staff College, 1983), 24-26.

[53] Kwak, Pattersen, and Olsen, *The Two Koreas in World Politics*: 333-34.

In 1969, the Nixon administration was the first to attempt an alteration of the U.S. strength in Korea. The scrutiny of the Vietnam War exacerbated by domestic sentiment of the U.S. as the "world's policeman" intensified President Nixon's desire to withdraw troops from Korea, despite his views on foreign policy dubbed, the Nixon Doctrine.[54] The Nixon Doctrine claimed that the U.S. would keep its treaty commitments to allies in the Far East, would continue to provide a nuclear umbrella to its allies, would provide a nuclear shield to countries deemed essential to U.S. national security, and encouraged friendly nations under military threat to defend their own country before seeking assistance.[55] The Nixon Doctrine asserted, "American allies must assume more of the responsibility in providing for their own defense and the broader security of the region."[56] The fledgling Republic of Korea did not have the economic influence that it enjoys today and required an outside source in defense of the country. However, the precariousness of North Korea juxtaposed with the Cold War required an U.S. military presence in Korea despite the Nixon Doctrine's desire for troop reduction. President Nixon agreed to provide economic aid and naval and air assistance but ordered the withdrawal of the Seventh Infantry Division leaving only the Second Infantry Division to supplement ROK ground forces. Political pressure to withdraw U.S. troops from Korea despite the uncertainty of the Cold War gave testament to the notion that even then the Republic of Korea was capable of assuming more responsibility for self-defense if given certain incentives. President Nixon was not the last to prove this point.

President Ford's administration seemed to distance themselves from their predecessor in promulgating sustained troop strength in South Korea. Although the scope of this monograph is

---

[54] Berry and Army War College (U.S.) Strategic Studies Institute., *The Invitation to Struggle: Executive and Legislative Competition Over the U.S. Military Presence on the Korean Peninsula*: 3.

[55] Jussi M. Hanhimäki, *The Flawed Architect: Henry Kissinger and American Foreign Policy* (New York: Oxford University Press, 2004), 53-54.

[56] Berry and Army War College (U.S.) Strategic Studies Institute., *The Invitation to Struggle: Executive and Legislative Competition Over the U.S. Military Presence on the Korean Peninsula*: 3.

not presidential personalities and relationships with advisors and cabinet members, it is important to recognize that Ford's Secretary of State, Henry Kissinger, had a very influential role in President Ford's foreign policy. Nixon had never allowed Kissinger to express his vision of realism to the press because of Nixon's own desire to appear authoritarian, while keeping his advisors out of the spotlight. With Ford however, Kissinger's vision of realism seemed more influential because of Ford's relative inexperience with foreign policy. This allowed Kissinger to project his own vision to the press, presenting his policies as policies of the President.[57] Therefore, the policy of the Ford administration was to maintain a prominent presence in Asia despite the situation in Vietnam and "the retention of combat ground forces in South Korea was a signal of American resolve to remain a force to be reckoned with in Asia."[58]

As much as the Ford administration affirmed America's commitment to South Korea, President Carter's administration placed a heavy strain on relations, further raising ROK fears of U.S. abandonment. Carter began touting troop reduction in Korea as early as his 1976 presidential campaign. A week after his inauguration, Carter issued orders to a policy review committee under the purview of the Department of State to review U.S. policy towards Korea.[59] The policy review concluded that South Korea could defend itself against North Korean aggression with U.S. air and naval support. By May 1977, President Carter ordered a troop reduction plan based on three reasons.[60] First, Carter believed that ROK ground forces had gained a substantial improvement over KPA ground forces since the Korea War, concluding it to be unnecessary for U.S. ground force supplementation.[61] Second, Carter surmised that U.S. relations with China and the Soviet

---

[57] Hanhimäki, *The Flawed Architect: Henry Kissinger and American Foreign Policy*: 291-301.

[58] Berry and Army War College (U.S.) Strategic Studies Institute., *The Invitation to Struggle: Executive and Legislative Competition Over the U.S. Military Presence on the Korean Peninsula*: 5.

[59] Lee, *A Troubled Peace: U.S. Policy and the Two Koreas*: 82.

[60] Berry and Army War College (U.S.) Strategic Studies Institute., *The Invitation to Struggle: Executive and Legislative Competition Over the U.S. Military Presence on the Korean Peninsula*: 6.

[61] Ibid., 7.

Union had vastly improved since the Korean War while Sino-Soviet relations deteriorated, making Soviet and Chinese support to a North Korean attack on South Korea unlikely.[62] Finally, Carter concluded, "South Korea was developing a strong economy and was fast approaching the time when it could provide for its own defense."[63] Carter attempted to assuage ROK discontent for the withdrawal plan by assuring the South Korean government the U.S. was prepared to honor fully the agreement in the 1953 Mutual Defense Treaty in the event of a North Korean attack.[64] The Carter withdrawal plan fomented outrage and dispute within congress and his own administration, resulting in the presidential reprimand and relief of USFK Chief of Staff, Major General John Singlaub for his public disapproval of the President's policy.[65] By the end of his administration, Carter was only able to withdraw approximately 3,000 troops, leaving the U.S. military strength in Korea around 37,000.[66]

The Reagan and H.W. Bush administrations strongly opposed troop reductions in Korea. President Reagan believed, "a withdrawal would impede progress in achieving important American political and security interest [in the region]."[67] However, a looming economic crisis in the United States placed pressure on President George H.W. Bush to re-address the issue of force reduction in Korea. With the Cold War ending, changing perception of an Asian threat, and budgetary concerns on the rise, three U.S. senators introduced legislation that would reduce troop strength in Korea by 10,000 over three years.[68] The Pentagon estimated in a1989 study that the

---

[62] Ibid, 7.

[63] Ibid, 7.

[64] Lee, *A Troubled Peace: U.S. Policy and the Two Koreas*: 87.

[65] Oberdorfer, *The Two Koreas: A Contemporary History*: 90.

[66] Ibid., 108.

[67] Berry and Army War College (U.S.) Strategic Studies Institute., *The Invitation to Struggle: Executive and Legislative Competition Over the U.S. Military Presence on the Korean Peninsula*: 11.

[68] Ibid., 12.

U.S. spent $2.6 billion annually to maintain troop strength in Korea.[69] The bill never became law, but changed American perception that a broad, global military presence was an unnecessary expenditure in light of rising deficits and the waning Cold War.[70]

By the mid-1990s and President Clinton's first term, the discussion for troop reduction in Korea dissipated due to an increased North Korean threat. The perception of North Korea as a nuclear threat emerged during the 1990's, further justifying the existence of U.S. forces in the ROK. Since the Korean War, President George W. Bush illustrated North Korea as a more significant threat than any previous administration. In President Bush's 2002 State of the Union address, he labeled North Korea as part of an "axis of evil" with Iran and Iraq, portending them to be serious threats to national security. However, the duration and requirements of the wars in Iraq and Afghanistan overshadowed the necessity for increased troop strength in the ROK. Secretary of Defense Donald Rumsfeld's 2004 plan to reduce and relocate U.S. troop strength in Korea in order to free up resources for Iraq and Afghanistan demonstrate the possibility to maintain stability on the Korean Peninsula with a reduced military posture. Rumsfeld's plan permanently removed one combat brigade from the Second Infantry Division, leaving one heavy brigade combat team in Korea and an overall strength of 28,500 troops in 2008.[71]

Operational Environment Conclusion

America's abiding concern in the security and welfare of South Korea is intrinsically tied to the two nations' shared history. Before this relationship began, the Korean people had suffered at the hands of outsiders, especially from Japan's brutal occupation from 1905 until the end of World War II. Sadly, the suffering did not end with the end of the war but merely transformed

---

[69] Ibid, 12.

[70] Ibid, 12.

[71] Mark E. Manyin et al., *U.S.-South Korea Relations: CRS Report for Congress* (Washington, D.C.: Congressional Research Service, Library of Congress, 2011), 19-20.

with the artificial division of the peninsular nation by the war's victors. The Truman Doctrine and America's policy to prevent the spread of communism codified a lasting role in South Korea's survival as the Cold War heated into the Korean War in 1950.[72] The 1953 Mutual Defense Treaty between the ROK and U.S. assured military assistance in the event of an attack on South Korea by a third party. The treaty justified U.S. presence in Korea, but it did not mandate permanency. America had successfully deterred the spread of communism into the ROK through the Soviet Union's collapse. North Korea's recalcitrance prevented them from following their communist brothers' lead, justifying continued U.S. presence. However, this did not deter the debate to withdraw troops within American politics. Politicians have withdrawn or maintained troops in Korea despite the threat from the north. Even after North Korea attained the stature as a nuclear threat, troop strength fluctuated in the ROK. President Bush's description of North Korea as an "axis of evil" certainly should have solidified a necessity for sustained troop strength to deter hostilities, however, more important interests abroad required the U.S. to downsize in Korea, once again. The background and history of the operational environment indicates that the U.S. and ROK can sustain their political ends regardless of fluctuating ways and means. In other words, the combined efforts of both countries have and continue to deter North Korean aggression despite the debate over the appropriate expenditure of U.S. tax dollars and the maintenance of a specific troop level. This opens the discussion for more cost-effective ways and means to achieve stability in Korea as it relates to the ROK's steady rise to prosperity and America's climbing debt.

---

[72] Lee, *A Troubled Peace: U.S. Policy and the Two Koreas*: 24.

Character of the Threat and Friendly Force

Satellite pictures from space portray the vast differences in prosperity of the two Koreas since their separation in 1945. The dark, lifeless mass of land that makes up North Korea compared to the vibrant, illuminated cities of South Korea provides an indication between the economic disparities of the two Koreas. In the north, the illumination of Pyongyang, the DPRK's capital city, indicates the resources of the entire country exist to support the government. More likely, all of North Korea's resources go to the support and survival of their oppressive governing regime instead of the care and prosperity of the people. In contrast, South Korea appears to have blossomed in prosperity with electricity illuminating the capital city and other major and minor cities throughout the country. Since the division of the two Koreas, the Republic of Korea has grown to become the fifteenth largest economy in the world trading largely with her neighbors China and Japan, the second and third largest economies in the world. The outlier in the region,

Democratic People's Republic of Korea, endures one of the weakest economies in the world while threatening the stability of the entire region.[73]

Economic prosperity and stability within Northeast Asia ultimately affect economic markets around the world. The United States benefits from security in the region, and it is in their best interests to invest in that security and stability. However, the U.S. must consider the balance of military capabilities between the two Koreas in order to determine what investments they need to provide in order to preserve stability. The strategy of out-buying the enemy during the cold war does not apply in the twenty-first century against rogue and isolated states like North Korea. The United States has always been the world leader in military technology and spending. However, as North Korea emerges more as an asymmetric threat, the U.S. must find more cost effective solutions to counter that threat. The innovation and tactics used by asymmetric and irregular forces tend to disrupt the superiority of U.S. military power.[74] U.S. and ROK policy makers cannot assume that U.S. military presence is the only stabilizer in the region and suppressor of North Korean belligerence. Furthermore, understanding what the U.S. military provides in order to preserve stability helps identify shortfalls in ROK military capabilities in the absence of U.S. presence.

Character of the Threat: North Korea

Ends:

North Korea remains a threat to regional and global stability through belligerence and nuclear weapons proliferation. Their leader between 1994 and 2011, Kim Jong-Il, died on December 17, 2011. Prior to his death, his ultimate strategic goal was the survival of his regime. Kim's third son and successor, Kim Jong-un, has shown no indication of changing the strategic

---

[73] *The Economist Pocket World in Figures, 2011 Edition.*

[74] U.S. Department of Defense, "The 2010 Quadrennial Defense Review," (U.S. Department of Defense, 2010), 80.

end state since his father's death. The Kim family regime has been able to maintain power in North Korea by maintaining control over the population and preventing external powers from influencing or affecting their interest and have been able to accomplish this by depriving their people from contact to the outside world and perpetuating fear of a military attack by U.S. and ROK forces. This justifies to their people a focus and emphasis on a strong military, ensuring the resources of the nation first go to the maintenance and strength of the military. North Korea has also focused on an asymmetric warfare capability while continuing a nuclear weapons program to supplement an inferior conventional fighting force.[75]

Ways and Means:

The DPRK maintains the fourth largest military in the world behind China, the United States, and India. Despite a vast fleet of antiquated relics of Cold War era Soviet made armor, North Korea keeps over 21,000 artillery guns of different capabilities and calibers that can range far beyond the southern outskirts of South Korea's capital city and well within the range of a majority of U.S. bases. Comparatively, South Korea only maintains a little over 11,000 artillery pieces of aging technology despite the threat from the north.[76] North Korea also maintains the largest Special Operations Force in the world with nearly 200,000 specialized soldiers.[77] The genesis of North Korea's assessment of a more robust Special Operations Forces comes from an internal strategic study of U.S. military actions in Operation Desert Storm compared to the asymmetric effects on U.S. forces in Operations Iraqi Freedom and Enduring Freedom. The study also advocated long-range rocket artillery and ballistic missiles, electronic intelligence warfare

---

[75] Sharp, "Statement of General Walter L. Sharp Commander, United Nations Command; Commander, United States-Republic of Korea Combined Forces Command; and Commander, United States Forces Korea Before the House Armed Services Committee, April 6, 2011," 6-9.

[76] *The Military Balance, 2011*, IISS publication (London,: International Institute for Strategic Studies, 2011), 205-54.

[77] Blain Harden, "North Korea Massively Increases Its Special Forces," *The Washington Post*, October 9, 2009. http://www.washingtonpost.com/wpdyn/content/article/2009/10/08/AR2009 100804018.html (accessed March 1, 2012).

capabilities, a more flexible reserve force, and a lighter, more mobile ground force to supplement asymmetric capabilities aimed at countering U.S. and ROK capabilities.

North Korea has tested these asymmetric capabilities against the south and achieved better awareness of ROK and U.S. capabilities at minimal expense to their own forces. In September 1996, a North Korean submarine infiltrated into waters off South Korea's east coast and struck ground on a reef close to shore. A combination of North Korean naval submariners and Special Forces infiltrators comprised a twenty-six man element that proceeded to evade through South Korea. Their mission started as a simple reconnaissance operation that turned into a hostile evasion after they were spotted and compromised by a South Korean taxi driver. After several days of evasion, ROK forces captured one North Korean infiltrator, one escaped back to the north, and the rest either were killed or committed suicide. South Korea suffered sixteen soldiers and civilians killed and twenty-seven wounded, but the fear and internal questioning of ROK military preparedness exacerbated diplomatic relations between the north and south and revealed ROK and U.S. inability to deter and counter asymmetric threats.[78]

The most dangerous and prolific threat that North Korea projects onto the ROK/U.S. alliance and the rest of the world is their ability to develop and test nuclear weapons and missiles that could range close to U.S. borders. The George W. Bush administration did little to ease tensions with North Korea when it declared the DPRK a member of an "axis of evil" with Iraq and Iran in early 2002.[79] The Bush administration justified a 2003 military invasion into Iraq to overthrow the Hussein regime for their noncompliance with a U.N. resolution to discontinue weapons-grade nuclear production. The late Kim Jong-Il interpreted U.S. bellicosity as a justification to expedite his own nuclear efforts while strengthening his asymmetric capabilities in

---

[78] Harry P. Dies Jr, "North Korean Special Operations Forces: 1996 Kangnung Submarine Infiltration," *Military Intelligence Professional Bulletin* 30, no. 4 (2004): 29-34.

[79] Lawrence Freedman, *Deterrence* (Cambridge, UK; Malden, MA: Polity Press, 2004), 98-99.

24

order to deter a possible invasion into his own country. He also used the case of the Libyan uprising in 2011 as a justification to continue his pursuit for nuclear weapons, believing that the U.S. would not intervene with nuclear states over domestic scuttles.[80] North Korea has always been able to use their nuclear ambitions as a bargaining chip to ease tensions with South Korea and receive financial and humanitarian aid when required. However, as administrations change in both the ROK and United States, policies toward North Korea differ in levels of severity depending on the administration.[81]

The Korean Peninsula remains a focal point for U.S. military intervention due to North Korea's unpredictable belligerence and U.S. and ROK's precarious policies towards the north based on the mood of administrations. A perpetual cycle of relaxed policies towards North Korea followed by heightened tensions by administrations justifies U.S. presence in South Korea while the DPRK uses the same fluctuation to justify their continued nuclear weapons program. Kim Jong-Il further justified his nuclear program prior to his death by referring to the United States' intervention in Libya even after they had abandoned their nuclear program many years ago, stating that he would not make the same mistake as the Libyans.[82] As nuclear endeavors led to stricter policies and sanctions toward the north, the DPRK attempted to coerce dialog with the south through deadly measures when it sank a ROK navy ship *Cheonan* and shelled the South Korean island of Yeonpyeong in 2010. Both incidents resulted in ROK civilian and military casualties with little to no consequences, other than a harsh censure from both ROK and U.S. administrations. Until the North Korean regime collapses from within, or the United States

---

[80] Mira Rapp-Hooper and Kenneth N. Waltz, "What Kim Jong-Il Learned from Qaddafi's Fall: Never Disarm," *The Atlantic* (2011). http://www.theatlantic.com/international/archive/2011/10/what-kim-jong-il-learned-from-qaddafis-fall-never-disarm/247192/ (accessed March 1, 2012).

[81] Council on Foreign Relations. Independent Task Force on U.S. Policy Toward the Korean Peninsula. et al., *U.S. Policy Toward the Korean Peninsula* (New York: Council on Foreign Relations, 2010), 3-5.

[82] Rapp-Hooper and Waltz, "What Kim Jong-Il Learned from Qaddafi's Fall: Never Disarm."

changes its policies toward them, the DPRK will remain a focal point for the U.S. military while spending, troops, and equipment continue to flow in South Korea.

Character of the Friendly Force: Republic of Korea

Ends:

The Republic of Korea has emerged as a global economic powerhouse since the dismal years of war with their brothers from the north followed by nearly three decades of identity and social "soul" searching that nearly ripped the nation into unmendable disparity. By 2011, South Korea prospered as the fifteenth largest economy in the world and survived the global financial crisis of the late 2000s as one of the only nations to rapidly recover and continue growth.[83] South Korea houses one of the world's top 25 largest cities that is headquarters to industrial powerhouses such as Samsung, LG, KIA, and Hyundai. Much of South Korea's financial success is derived from trade and exports mostly to China, the United States, and Japan. The ROK enjoys global recognition as host to the 1988 Summer Olympic Games, 2002 World Cup Soccer Championships, 2010 G-20 Summit, and home of the future 2018 Winter Olympic Games. Many of these titles have contributed to South Korea's economic success. Despite South Korea's growing economic prosperity, the percentage of gross domestic product they invest in their military, which stagnated at 2.6 percent in 2008, reflects their commitment to national defense.[84] It is questionable why a wealthy country with so many resources worth protecting would invest so little in their national security, but the relationship between the ROK and U.S. has created a dependency that allows the South Koreans to invest a relatively small portion of their national wealth in their national defense. However, South Korea and the United States share the same strategic ends concerning the South's security. Stability between the two Koreas and within the

---

[83] *The Economist Pocket World in Figures, 2011 Edition*: 24-31, 216-17.

[84] Ibid., 103.

region would allow South Korean prosperity to grow, while conflict would potentially hurt their economy.[85] Currently, the ways and means South Korea pursues to achieve their ends seems to be the responsibility of the U.S.

Ways and Means:

The notion that the United States should bear much of the security costs on the Korean Peninsula is a paradigm that has lasted since the Korean War, well before the ROK's economic success. This notion stems from the idea that since the United States has such a vested interest in the security and stability within Northeast Asia, and since it is a more powerful nation compared to South Korea, it should bear the majority of security costs on the peninsula. The South Korean view of the bilateral security relationship between the U.S. and ROK summarizes this notion:

> Initially, South Korea was a weak, underdeveloped nation that could not cope with the overwhelming threats of its communist neighbors by itself. South Korean dependence on the United States for its security was inevitable under these conditions. It was not a matter of choice, but a requirement for survival. The nation put aside its national pride and accepted a dominant-subservient alliance with the United States. During the Korean War, South Korea even conceded full operational control of its armed forces to the U.S. command.[86]

The ROK has focused its military investments on less expensive ground forces while deferring the more expensive naval and air power expenditures on to the United States because of this economic imbalance. The South Korean Armed Forces maintains a robust ground force of 522,000 soldiers that includes four armored brigades, five mechanized divisions, seventeen infantry divisions, and seven Special Forces brigades. Comparatively, the United States maintains only one heavy brigade combat team, a combat aviation brigade, and an artillery brigade

---

[85] The White House, "The 2010 National Security Strategy," (Washington, DC: GPO, 2010), 44.

[86] Robert A. Scalapino and Hongkoo Lee, *Korea-U.S. Relations: The Politics of Trade and Security*, Research Papers and Policy Studies (Berkeley: Institute of East Asian Studies, University of California, 1988), 205.

subordinate to the only infantry division headquarters in the ROK.[87] However, access to assistance from more extensive naval and air power, either stationed in the ROK or on a rotational basis, compensates for the lack of U.S. ground forces.

The ROK Navy employs 68,000 naval personnel to operate 23 tactical submarines, one cruiser, six destroyers, 12 frigates, 30 corvettes, and ten mine warfare ships. Included in these numbers is the ROK's 27,000 personnel marine force. The ROK Air Force maintains 65,000 airmen to operate their aging fleet of 490 combat capable aircraft comprised of, but not limited to, F-5B Freedom Fighters, F-4E Phantom IIs, F-16C and F-16D Fighting Falcons and C-130H Hercules cargo planes. A smaller navy and air force compared to a larger ground force is common in most militaries, however, the antiquated computer and weapons systems employed by ROK ships and planes have not kept up with modern technology and risk obsoleteness if costly investments are not made. In many cases, computer and weapons systems within ROK ships and planes are incompatible with more modern, albeit costly, systems in U.S. ships and planes. Although the USFK commander asserted to the U.S. Congress that, "it [ROK military] is a modern, mobile network centric warfare capable force that fields an array of advanced weapon systems," much of this technology is given to the ROK Army.[88] The U.S. provides the ROK military with the enablers needed to operate within the U.S. concept of network centric warfare. It is not a capability the ROK government provides to their own forces using their own funds. The ROK Air Force does not even have the capability to infiltrate their highly skilled and well trained Special Forces soldiers into North Korea if combat operations were to ensue because of the lack of costly infiltration platforms. This capability would most likely be deferred to U.S. Air Force

---

[87] Robert A. Scalapino and Hongkoo Lee, *Korea-U.S. Relations: The Politics of Trade and Security*, Research Papers and Policy Studies (Berkeley: Institute of East Asian Studies, University of California, 1988), 205.

[88] *The Military Balance, 2011*: 252-53.

assets subordinate to the Combined Forces Command with the capability to evade North Korean air defense measures.[89]

South Korean politicians seemingly limit ROK military preparedness, despite efforts to modernize the force. ROK military forces display their preparedness and ability to fight during three annual combined training exercises with U.S. forces and several unilateral exercises. Each exercise tests the range of combined military capabilities against a myriad of scenarios related to their North Korean neighbors. Each exercise is testament to the ROK military's ability to fight and win against a North Korean foe with the aid and assistance provided by superior U.S. technology and experience.[90]

Korean politics is central to the insufficient defense expenditures suffered by their military. Both North and South Korea benefited from a ROK policy during the 1990s and early 2000s known as the "sunshine" policy that opened up dialogue, tourism, and commerce between the two countries. Presidents Kim Dae-jung (1998-2003) and Roh Moo-hyun (2003-2008) embraced this policy as a cost-effective means to stabilize relations and deter military actions, justifying lower expenditures on national defense. President Roh even went so far as to support his presidential campaign with anti-American sentiments generated by the deaths of two Korean schoolchildren run over by U.S. military vehicles in 2002.[91] U.S. forces continue to endure these anti-American sentiments despite USFK efforts to improve relations with the South Korean people. However, the South Korean people have been encouraged to view the people of North Korea as "brothers and sisters" who are in great need of their help and not view them as the

---

[89] Sharp, "Statement of General Walter L. Sharp Commander, United Nations Command; Commander, United States-Republic of Korea Combined Forces Command; and Commander, United States Forces Korea Before the House Armed Services Committee, April 6, 2011."

[90] *The Military Balance, 2011.*

[91] Sharp, "Statement of General Walter L. Sharp Commander, United Nations Command; Commander, United States-Republic of Korea Combined Forces Command; and Commander, United States Forces Korea Before the House Armed Services Committee, April 6, 2011."

"enemy" as the Americans view the north. President Kim Dae-jung expressed these sentiments after a North-South summit meeting in Pyongyang in 2000. He also claimed that there would no longer be any war between the North and South because the North would not attempt to unify the two Koreas by force.[92] With sentiments like these, substantiated or not, anti-American sentiments and notions of close North and South Korean ties easily dissuade South Korean voters from supporting government policies that would direct more tax dollars (Korean won) towards the defense budget.

The other face of South Korean politics, the one disregarded by their people, is the one that fosters a strong military alliance with the United States. Despite the anti-American and pro-North Korean sentiments advertised by both aforementioned presidents, each president had maintained close support for U.S. military presence in their country. The genesis of South Korean pride comes from centuries of heritage that is based on a survival culture that has endured war, occupation, and division.[93] It is important for the Korean people to be able to display to the world their economic strength and prosperity to prove that they have endured and emerged from hardship.[94] The ROK President should maintain and promote the South Korean brand of pride and nationalism, while providing for the best interests of the taxpayers. South Korean branding attracts investors, trading partners, and buyers of South Korean products all over the world. Domestically, the South Korean brand has been promulgated through the before mentioned sporting venues and G-20 summit.[95] South Korean also demonstrates her strength abroad through their army's support of humanitarian assistance operations, United Nations peacekeeping operations, and training venues in Iraq, Afghanistan, East Timor, Haiti, India, Pakistan, Lebanon,

---

[92] Manyin et al., *U.S.-South Korea Relations: CRS Report for Congress,* 27-29.

[93] Norman D. Levin, *Do the Ties Still Bind?: The U.S.-ROK Security Relationship After 9/11* (Santa Monica, CA: Rand Corporation, 2004), 26.

[94] Chung Kiseon and Choe Hyun, "South Korean National Pride: Determinants, Changes, and Suggestions," *Asian Perspective* 32, no. 1 (2008): 122-23.

[95] Ibid., 116-20.

Nepal, United Arab Emirates, and Sudan.[96] South Korea enjoys the relatively inexpensive global recognition earned by their military at the cost of neglected defense expenditures on much needed long-range airborne infiltration platforms and aerial refueling capabilities, intelligence, surveillance, and reconnaissance platforms, and attack aviation; all of which are provided by American forces stationed in Korea or on a rotational basis.[97]

The cost to maintain 28,500 U.S. military troops in South Korea accumulated to nearly $3 billion in 2011. Of that, the ROK government contributed $743 million, 42 percent of the total cost. However, over $309.6 million of that money went to pay the salaries of the Korean national employees hired to work on U.S. military installations throughout Korea in service related jobs (i.e. retail and food services) and more technical occupations such as human resources, financier, librarian, and employees at the myriad of U.S. Army administrative offices located on U.S. garrisons. Over $128.5 million of that money was logistics related covering some supplies, logistics equipment, and services, while nearly $304.8 million went to construction costs related to consolidation of U.S. troops in Korea.[98] Ostensibly, of the $743 million the ROK government contributed to U.S. military costs in Korea, almost all of that money went back into the South Korean economy.

From an economic standpoint, South Korea is getting a great rate of return for less than three-quarters of a billion U.S. dollars. South Korea invests very little of its great wealth in its military because of the assurance of U.S. military protection in the event of increased hostilities. A 2004 Rand Corporation study highlights this point, stating,

> [I]f war were ever to come to the peninsula, the combat power deployed by
> the U.S. would in aggregate more than double South Korea's combat power.

---

[96] University of Southern California. Korean Studies Institute. and Korea Economic Institute (U.S.), *Towards Sustainable Economic & Security Relations in East Asia: U.S. and ROK Policy Options*, Joint U.S.-Korea Academic Studies (Washington, D.C.: Korea Economic Institute, 2008), 210-13.

[97] *The Military Balance, 2011*: 254.

[98] Levin, *Do the Ties Still Bind?: The U.S.-ROK Security Relationship After 9/11*: 13-14.

This additional power, moreover, would come from largely active duty, extremely well-trained U.S. personnel with equipment considerably better than Koreans could field on their own…Few countries have Korea's ability to rapidly draw on such enormous combat power at so little expense in peacetime. If Korea had to replicate this power itself, the impact would resonate throughout South Korean society.[99]

The South Korean people witnessed the commitment and readiness of U.S. military assistance in the immediate aftermath of two unprovoked North Korean attacks in 2010.[100] The March 2010 sinking of a South Korean Navy ship by a North Korean torpedo resulted in a combined ROK/U.S. maritime and air readiness-training event off the east coast of Korea and combined anti-submarine warfare training exercise shortly after an artillery exchange between North and South Korean forces on the island of Yeongpyeong in November 2010.[101] These combined training events were in addition to three annual combined exercises, and were designed to pacify North Korean belligerence and display effective U.S./ROK rapid response with military assets from the Korean Peninsula and other locations.[102]

Character of the Friendly Force: United States

The environment for which the U.S. military operates has come under greater fiscal scrutiny since terrorists attacked the United States on September 11, 2001. The wars in Afghanistan and Iraq have required higher troop strengths and equipment purchases while defense spending reached its highest point since World War II with a budget request of over 676

---

[99] Sharp, "Statement of General Walter L. Sharp Commander, United Nations Command; Commander, United States-Republic of Korea Combined Forces Command; and Commander, United States Forces Korea Before the House Armed Services Committee, April 6, 2011."

[100] Levin, *Do the Ties Still Bind?: The U.S.-ROK Security Relationship After 9/11*: 12.

[101] Cordesman and Gagel, *The Korean Military Balance: Comparative Korean Forces and the Forces of Key Neighboring States: Main Report*: 71.

[102] Sharp, "Statement of General Walter L. Sharp Commander, United Nations Command; Commander, United States-Republic of Korea Combined Forces Command; and Commander, United States Forces Korea Before the House Armed Services Committee, April 6, 2011," 5.

billion U.S. dollars for fiscal year 2012.[103] In 2011, the U.S. economy remained the largest in the world with the greatest purchasing power, however, they were ranked 30th in the world for the lowest economic growth while South Korea ranked 51st in the world for the highest economic growth.[104] Despite a high wealth status, in 2008 the United States suffered their worst financial and economic crisis since the Great Depression.[105] The September 2001 attacks exacerbated an incipient economic recession while irresponsible bank lending and home mortgage borrowing could not keep up with Americans' weakening paychecks.[106] Scrutiny over high defense spending stemmed from this strained fiscal environment, while debate over the prosecution of the war on terror questioned increases in the defense budget. An independent 2010 U.S. country review bluntly described the fiscal environment stating, "the federal budget balance has turned from a surplus of US$128 billion in 2001 to continued deficits since 2002 because of tax cuts and growing spending on military and homeland security. The budget deficit reached US$413 billion in 2004, or 3.6 percent of GDP, due to spiraling costs of national security, the war on terrorism and the war in Iraq."[107]

The decline in U.S. economic growth has caused many policy makers to propose reductions in the federal deficit by cutting taxes and reduce federal spending. Much of this reduction in federal spending would come from the defense budget. The defense budget grew annually in real terms by $300 billion between fiscal years 2001 and 2011, attributing much of the increase to the global war on terrorism, military pay and benefits, peacetime operating costs,

---

[103] Ibid., 11-14.

[104] Todd Harrison, "Analysis of the FY 2012 Defense Budget," (Center for Strategic and Budgetary Assessments, 2011), v.

[105] *The Economist Pocket World in Figures, 2011 Edition*: 24, 30.

[106] "Economic Overview," in *United States Country Review* (CountryWatch Incorporated, 2010), 374.

[107] Ibid., 373-74; James K. Galbraith, "On the Economics of Deficits," *American Prospect* 21, no. 9 (2010).

and modernization and replacement of weapon systems.[108] Despite the overall growth in the

defense budget, some pundits say that the capabilities of the force have not grown with defense

spending. Defense analyst, Todd Harrison, stated in an analysis of the 2012 defense budget that,

> Overall, nearly half of the growth in defense spending over the past decade
> is unrelated to the wars in Afghanistan and Iraq – personnel costs grew
> while end strength remained relatively flat, the cost of peacetime operations
> grew while the pace of peacetime operations declined, and acquisition costs
> increased while the inventory of equipment grew smaller and older. The
> base budget now supports a force with essentially the same size, force
> structure, and capabilities as in FY 2001 but at a 35 percent higher cost. The
> Department [of Defense] is spending more but not getting more.[109]

Likewise, the U.S. has reduced it forces in Korea by very little since 2001 and currently

maintains over 28,000 troops on the peninsula. As greater scrutiny is placed on the Defense

Department over dollars spent per capabilities earned, more scrutiny should be placed on U.S.

military presence in Korea. The U.S. force structure in Korea is equipped and organized for Cold

War tactics, though the fact remains that North Korea has not launched a full-scale attack on

South Korea or begun a new chapter in the Korean War since U.S. forces placed permanent

posting on the peninsula.

Ends:

The National Security Strategy guides military planning to achieve a certain condition

within an operating environment.[110] The *2010 National Security Strategy* aims to build sources of

American strength and influence and shape international order in the best interests of their way of

life.[111] Stability and security in Northeast Asia is of great concern for the United States since

much of the world's economic throughput originates from that region. Specifically, the National

Security Strategy identifies South Korea as a partner nation that is "the bedrock of security in

---

[108] "Economic Overview," 374.

[109] Harrison, "Analysis of the FY 2012 Defense Budget," vi.

[110] Ibid.

[111] Department of the Army, *FM 5-0: The Operations Process*, ed. Department of the Army (Washington, DC: GPO, 2010), 2-14, 2-15.

Asia and a foundation of prosperity in the Asia-Pacific region" and vows to continue to "deepen and update" this alliance to keep up with changing and emerging security trends of the 21st century.[112] The daunting challenge of shaping international order is not the sole responsibility of the United States. The U.S. recognizes this fact, as do many other nations who are taking on more powerful regional and global stability roles as their nations achieve greater economic and political stability. U.S. security strategy aims to harness this cooperation for the greater global good and states, "we are, therefore, deepening our partnerships with emerging powers and encouraging them to play a greater role in strengthening international norms and advancing shared interest."[113] How the U.S. Defense Department and military services interpret this strategic vision must reflect the emerging economic environment and utilize cost-effective ways and means to achieve the strategic ends.

Ways and Means:

The Department of Defense's *2008 National Defense Strategy* envisions the strategic environment as a "global struggle against a violent extremist ideology that seeks to overturn the international state system."[114] This document lays out the ways for which military strategists and operational planners seek to implement the ways for U.S. forces to pursue strategic ends. Predominantly, this vision focuses on emerging global asymmetric and irregular threats, but also accounts for the dangers of failing and rogue states and the proliferation of weapons of mass destruction. The defense strategy pays particular attention to North Korea's potential for nuclear and missile proliferation and portends, "[t]he regime threatens the Republic of Korea with its military and its neighbors with its missiles. Moreover, North Korea creates instability with its illicit activity, such as counterfeiting U.S. currency and trafficking in narcotics, and brutal

---

[112] The White House, "The 2010 National Security Strategy," 42.

[113] Ibid., 42.

[114] Department of Defense, "The 2008 National Defense Strategy," (Washington, DC: GPO, 2008), 2.

35

treatment of its own people."[115] The ways the U.S. seeks to maintain stability in the region is by deterring North Korean aggression and preventing the spread of weapons of mass destruction. The means for which the U.S. fulfills the ways of pursuing the strategic ends is through a robust military presence that has pervaded in South Korea since the end of the Korean War. The 28,500 U.S. military personnel that comprise the United States Forces Korea Command come from the 8th Army Headquarters, 2nd Infantry Division, 7th Air Force, 19th Expeditionary Sustainment Command, Naval Forces Korea, Marine Forces Korea, and Special Operations Command Korea. Their mission to defend the Republic of Korea against external aggression and maintain peace and stability in East Asia has not changed since the end of the Korean War.[116] The technology, firepower, and expertise U.S. forces contribute to the Combined Forces Command would be effective in a conventional fight but has had no consequence to North Korea's pursuit for nuclear weapons.[117] Although U.S. forces in Korea make up a very small percentage of the entire military, their permanency in Korea does not allow these forces to be deployed elsewhere in the world regardless of how much they are needed.[118]

The Way Ahead

Advocating a smaller U.S. military structure in Korea is a seemingly difficult task considering strong political support from both Congress and the White House to maintain a

---

[115] Ibid., 3.

[116] "United States Forces Korea," USFK Public Affairs, http://www.usfk.mil/usfk/ (accessed December 10, 2011).

[117] John P. Cummings, "Should the U.S. Continue to Maintain Forces in South Korea?," (Carlisle Barracks, PA: U.S. Army War College, 2004), 11.

[118] One brigade combat team deployed from the 2nd Infantry Division in support of Operation Iraqi Freedom, but did not return to garrison in Korea. Likewise, an AH-64 battalion deployed to Afghanistan and did not return to South Korea. Individual augmentees have also deployed from Korea in support of OIF and OEF. Current efforts by the Department of Defense to allow units to deploy from Korea have been stifled by Congress.

presence in the region.[119] In January 2012, President Obama announced a reduction in defense

spending while directing priorities for future defense endeavors in the Asian-Pacific region.

Recent defense guidance outlined these priorities, stating,

> Our relationships with Asian allies and key partners are critical to the future stability and growth of the region. We will emphasize our existing alliances, which provide a vital foundation for Asian-Pacific security. We will also expand our networks of cooperation with emerging partners throughout the Asian-Pacific to ensure collective capability and capacity for securing common interests…Furthermore, we will maintain peace on the Korean Peninsula by effectively working with allies and other regional states to deter and defend against provocation from North Korea, which is actively pursuing a nuclear weapons program.[120]

The Defense Department will reduce future expenditures by nearly $487 billion over the

next ten years on top of a self-imposed reduction of $100 billion directed by former Secretary

Gates in 2011.[121] This will place greater burden on the military services to cut spending in less

effective programs, excess and underused personnel, and require smarter investing in future

weapon systems and technology. Likewise, military planners will have to maximize the use of

existing forces and equipment to counter losses due to budget cuts. The Defense Department

claims that these budget cuts are manageable because the remaining military force, albeit smaller

and leaner, "will remain agile, flexible, ready, innovative, and technologically advanced."[122]

Seemingly, the United States is at a decision point where the military is under a

constrained fiscal environment while emphasizing efforts in the Asian-Pacific region.

Understanding that defense dollars are limited, the U.S. will have to decide where they can make

the most of their investments and consider an increase in advisory capacity while limiting or

---

[119] Levin, "Hearing to Receive Testimony on U.S. Pacific Command and U.S. Forces Korea in Review of the Defense Authorization Request for Fiscal Year 2012 and the Future Years Defense Program."

[120] Department of Defense, "Sustaining U.S. Global Leadership: Priorities for 21st Century Defense," 1-2.

[121] United States, *Budget Control Act of 2011* (Washington, DC: GPO, 2011).

[122] Department of Defense, "Defense Budget Priorities and Choices." (Washington, DC: GPO, 2012).

reducing conventional ground force capability, invest in smarter technology, rely on the status quo, or a combination of several options. Expense reduction in personnel and under-performing programs while investing in smarter technology is not the only solution the Defense establishment should seek. Concerning Korea, military planners will also have to consider reducing the size of the force while maximizing the use of a smaller force structure. Regardless of how much money South Korea contributes to maintaining U.S. forces in Korea, overall costs in U.S. military expenditures will likely decrease with fewer forces. This will help contribute to the reduction in future defense spending. Military planners will have to use a better design methodology in order to develop a design concept that addresses the need to reduce forces in Korea, considering the declining budget, while developing a solution that maximizes the use of a lesser force. [123]

Understanding how relevant actors, tendencies, potentials, desired end state, and conditions relate to each other forms the basis of the problem frame. Understanding and isolating the root causes of conflict within that environment is key to problem framing. [124] Although cuts in funding for U.S. forces in Korea as part of the $487 billion reduction in defense spending is yet to be determined, this added variable could potentially be a driver for force restructuring even though U.S. strategy will focus more on the Asian-Pacific region. This proposed problem statement could clearly define the problem yet to be solved: how can U.S. military forces maintain stability on the Korean Peninsula while reducing force strengths and expenditures in the country?

---

[123] In accordance with *Field Manual 5-0, 2010,* U.S. Army design methodology seeks to produce a design concept by framing the environment, problem, and operational approach (solution). The goals of design are to understand ill-structured problem, anticipate change, create opportunities, and recognize and manage transitions.

[124] Army, *FM 5-0: The Operations Process*: 3-8 - 3-11.

Developing a potential solution requires considering operational approaches that can best achieve the desired condition or end state.[125] The White House's focus on the Asian-Pacific region justifies current troop levels in Korea while advocating further spending. However, military leaders, as good stewards of taxpayer's dollars, must prove they are truly innovative, agile, and adaptive in order to get the most gain for the least expense in achieving America's interests in Korea. The "Priorities for 21st Century Defense" seemingly advocates the status quo on the Korean Peninsula, allowing military planners to maintain a conventional-minded force. This mindset for the status quo will ultimately have consequences that increase defense spending in Korea while 28,500 troops defend a nation that has the wealth, innovation, and resources to defend it on their own. The prudent military planner should apply the fundamentals of design and understand that those forces could be better utilized in emerging global problem areas and advocate for an increased responsibility for South Korean forces by shifting more of the defense burden to them.[126]

Regardless, any decision the U.S. makes to future military investments or restructuring in South Korea comes with inherent risks as well as undeniable benefits. There are a myriad of possible approaches that range from great benefits for the U.S., increased risk for the ROK to great benefits for the ROK, increased risk for the U.S., and any combination in between. The following analysis examines two possible courses of action that lie closer to the center of the range of possible solutions. The first considers the risks and benefits of maintaining the status quo from the perspective that current policies and future budgeted programs for U.S. military forces in the ROK will continue as planned while achieving Congress's plan for reduced defense spending and the President's vision of increased focus in the Asian-Pacific region. The second considers an

---

[125] Ibid., 3-11.

[126] *FM 5-0* describes the fundamentals of design as applying critical thinking, understanding the operational environment, solving the right problem, adapt to dynamic conditions, and achieve the designated goals.

approach that balances the risks and benefits of shifting more of the defense burden on to the ROK while limiting the type of U.S. forces in South Korea and redefining their mission. This approach includes an expectation that the government of South Korea procures more and better technology for their defense either by sales from the U.S. and other allies or producing it from within their own industrial base.

Maintaining the Status Quo

U.S. forces have been postured in the ROK to repel a conventional North Korean attack since the end of the Korean War. As stated by a former USFK Commander, "American commitment [to ROK security] is demonstrated by an enduring force presence, the tour normalization initiative, provision of bridging and enduring capabilities, supply of augmentation forces in contingencies, and the continued provision of extended deterrence."[127] This statement not only summarizes the ways and means of maintaining stability in Korea, but also outlines the future for the status quo. This option of maintaining the status quo aims to preserve an enduring U.S. force presence in the ROK with continued projection for base consolidation and transfer of operational control of ROK forces to the ROK by 2015. The status quo is likely to commit increasing U.S. defense spending in the ROK while sharing the cost of relocating U.S. forces within the country. This approach, inherently, comes with both benefits and risks to the U.S. and the ROK.

The greatest benefit provided to both the U.S. and the Republic of Korea by maintaining the status quo is maintenance of the strong alliance between the two countries. Since World War II, the ROK remains one of the U.S.' closest allies and fought along side them in every major contingency from the Korean and Vietnam Wars to the wars in Iraq and Afghanistan. Containing

---

[127] Sharp, "Statement of General Walter L. Sharp Commander, United Nations Command; Commander, United States-Republic of Korea Combined Forces Command; and Commander, United States Forces Korea Before the House Armed Services Committee, April 6, 2011."

North Korean nuclear prospects is very important to U.S. interests, and an enduring U.S. force

presence ensures a strong U.S./ROK alliance in the event North Korean prospects turn into an all

out war.[128]

A significant additional benefit to the U.S. is the potential to utilize South Korean basing

as staging areas for further endeavors in the Asian-Pacific region. As mentioned earlier in this

paper, the Korean Peninsula served as a bridge for military forces between Sino-Japanese affairs

in early Korean history. Presence in South Korea serves as a vantage point for U.S. forces as

interests and relations between the United States and China continue to evolve.[129] However, the

defense of South Korea is priority number one for troops stationed there. Deploying them to other

regions of the world to partake in overseas contingency operations remains unlikely with

continued North Korean belligerence.

For the republic of Korea, the continued presence of significant U.S. forces provides

many benefits, not the least of which is the role that the presence of American troops plays in

maintaining the terms of the Armistice agreement, under the auspices of the UN. Another

significant benefit to the ROK for maintaining the status quo is the continued infusion of U.S.

dollars into the Korean economy and the ability for the ROK government to focus their own

spending on the continuing growth of that economy. This benefit to the ROK also serves as the

greatest risk to the U.S. if economic trends continue.

The greatest risk in maintaining the status quo is the strain that the cost of keeping forces

on the peninsula continues to place on the American economy. Further, if America's forces are

present during a future reunification of the two Koreas, the United States would likely be

expected to bear some of the financial burden of facilitating that reunification, driving the U.S.

---

[128] Levin, *Do the Ties Still Bind?: The U.S.-ROK Security Relationship After 9/11*: 39-45.

[129] Levin, "Hearing to Receive Testimony on U.S. Pacific Command and U.S. Forces Korea in Review of the Defense Authorization Request for Fiscal Year 2012 and the Future Years Defense Program," 14-17.

further into debt. Although it is undetermined exactly what percentage of reunification the U.S. would have to pay, estimates place the overall costs towards the high end, at nearly $700 billion.[130] The United States' share of reunification plus nearly $3 billion of annual costs to maintain U.S. forces in South Korea add to the burden of expected American assistance in the event of a North Korean regime collapse.

Shifting the Burden

Stability and security on the Korean Peninsula is a shared responsibility between the U.S. and ROK. Although the Unites States has stated a focus on the Asian-Pacific region, stability on the Korean Peninsula needs to be a majority concern for South Korea. The financial expenses and manpower the U.S commits to stability on the Korean Peninsula can be viewed as a burden instead of an investment, considering South Korea's economic prosperity. Shifting the majority of this burden to the South Korean people will allow the U.S. to decrease their military footprint on the peninsula. Decreasing U.S. military footprint and shifting more of the burden of defense to the Korean people will not only require the ROK to incur more unwanted defense spending, an alternative strategy for remaining U.S. forces will have to be addressed. Like the status quo, this option contains both risks and benefits.

Deterioration in the strong U.S./ROK alliance is a potential risk for the U.S., especially in light of President Obama's increased emphasis on the region. Not only has the ROK been one of the U.S.' closest allies since World War II, the U.S. also served as their closest trading partner until 2003, when China surpassed the U.S. as South Korea's closest trading partner.[131] China's

---

[130] Charles Wolf Jr, "Korean Reunification: How it Might Come About and at What Cost," *Defence & Peace Economics* 17, no. 6 (2006): 684-688.

[131] Manyin et al., *U.S.-South Korea Relations: CRS Report for Congress*, 17.

growing financial influence within the ROK could cause their political and military interests to align more closely if the U.S. were to leave completely the burden of defense to the ROK.[132]

Likewise, U.S. presence in the ROK has seemingly been a major factor in deterring an invasion of North Korea by the ROK and vice versa.[133] A significant reduction in U.S. presence on the peninsula could weaken this deterrent effort, which could lead to the significant costs associated with a force deployment to intervene in a violent reunification of the two Koreas.

As this paper has already determined that U.S. forces in Korea are postured for conventional conflict with North Korea, the emerging asymmetric capability requires a combined force that can counter this kind of threat. Focusing on maintaining a U.S. force presence that maximize South Korean capabilities vice offensive or defensive operations will allow for a reduced footprint while maintaining stability in the region. This construct would require U.S. forces to shift from a combat posture to more of an advisory role focused on Security Force Assistance (SFA) with their Korean counterparts. SFA aims to improve the capability and capacity of host-nation security forces across the full spectrum of conflict while placing little emphasis on offensive or defensive operations.[134] More and better advising to an already robust and capable ROK military will allow the alliance to better deflect North Korea's emerging asymmetric and irregular aspirations. This focus on building a better U.S. advisory force in Korea benefits the U.S. in that it could focus forces currently stationed there to other regions of interest or conflict.

Although the ROK maintains a technological advantage over their North Korean adversary, a significant shift in the security burden to their forces requires the further acquisition of technology to maintain the cutting edge in 21st century warfare. This requirement is potentially

---

[132] Levin, *Do the Ties Still Bind?: The U.S.-ROK Security Relationship After 9/11*: 42-44.

[133] Ibid.

[134] Department of the Army, *FM 3-07.1: Security Force Assistance* (Washington, DC: GPO, 2009), 1-1.

beneficial to the U.S., both in the ability to provide this technological edge to ROK forces through U.S. Foreign Military Sales, which will likely inject more money into the U.S. economy, and in the increase such sales create in the interoperability of both nations' military forces. The U.S. and ROK would have to coordinate closely to determine the types and quantities of technologies to be shared.

Although shifting more of the defense burden onto South Korea while increasing Foreign Military Sales and focusing remaining U.S. forces on SFA is not the only alternative to maintaining the current force structure in Korea, it provides a good start to addressing U.S. force commitment and economic issues and provides a point for further innovation and creativity. The age of seemingly endless defense dollars has ended and the U.S. military must adapt to this changed environment while pursuing U.S. security objectives. This approach helps fulfill guidance outlined in *Sustaining U.S. Global Leadership,* "Whenever possible, we will develop innovative, low-cost, and small-footprint approaches to achieve our security objectives, relying on exercises, rotational presence, and advisory capabilities."[135] This approach should also aspire to turn South Korea into a producer of security rather than a consumer of it as pointed out of America's European allies in the same 2012 defense guidance.

Analysis

The preceding segments have outlined only some of the risks and benefits to the ROK and U.S. in forging a regional security for the 21st century. Shifting the defense burden implies increased spending for the ROK and increased savings for the U.S., while maintaining the status quo implies continued spending for the U.S. and deferred investments for the ROK. However,

---

[135] Department of Defense, "Sustaining U.S. Global Leadership: Priorities for 21st Century Defense," 3.

agile, flexible, and innovative solutions will allow the U.S. to leverage a reduced defense budget with increased focus on the Asian-Pacific region.

The hundreds of billions of U.S. dollars spent to preserve stability to date will only increase by maintaining the status quo. The mentioned tour normalization initiative alone, if approved by Congress, will commit an additional $10.7 billion up thru 2020 to the already rising costs of U.S. force presence and an extra $15.7 billion between 2021 and 2050.[136] The initiative would eliminate unaccompanied tours in Korea and change the status from forward-deployed to forward-stationed with family members.[137] While raising the price tag for troops in Korea, this initiative comes with a host of other problems. Living space is limited in Korea, so are jobs for family members who seek employment through USFK, which favors Korean nationals by virtue of the Status of Forces Agreement. As U.S. military leaders and politicians portend North Korea to be an unpredictable threat to U.S. interests and the Republic of Korea, reducing force presence would minimize the number of family members potentially at risk.

Likewise, ten years of conflict in Afghanistan and Iraq have placed great stresses on U.S. military forces in terms of economics, retention, maintenance, and global flexibility. U.S. military options to intervene in the Arab world during uprisings against oppressive regimes in late 2010 and the ongoing situation in Syria have been limited partly because of the decade long war against terror. Military options become more strained in the future as the defense budget and force size continues to decrease and the peninsula continues to require the current level of American commitment. Shifting more of the defense burden to the ROK can help alleviate this.

The greatest benefactor of the status quo is the Republic of Korea. Even though ten years of war has taken its toll on U.S. forces, America continues to defend South Korea with money,

---

[136] "Defense Management: Comprehensive Cost Information and Analysis of Alternatives Needed to Assess Military," *GAO Reports* (2011): 9-15.

[137] Department of Defense, "The 2010 Quadrennial Defense Review," 52.

troops, and materiel while the ROK defers its own investment in the capabilities the U.S provides. U.S. military presence in Korea reduces ROK military defense spending while contributing to their overall economic development.[138] If the U.S. were to shift more of the security responsibility to the South Koreans, not only would the ROK have to replace provided equipment, they would also have to incur the added costs of maintaining and replacing aging systems. However, they would also gain economically in through investments in their own defense industries, and through the employment of people to work in the additional factories, facilities, and depots associated with this new equipment.

More study is needed to fully explore the potential risk of South Korean alignment with China associated with a reduced U.S. presence, even though this option does not consider removing all U.S. forces from the ROK. However, both the U.S. and ROK can benefit greatly from a shifting of security responsibilities—the U.S. from potential financial savings and force preservation, and the ROK from long-deferred investments in their own defense industries and military force capabilities.

Conclusion

While the 1953 Mutual Defense Treaty and 2009 Joint Vision Statement has solidified U.S. force presence in Korea, America continues to suffer from the effects of the economic crisis during the late 2000s while South Korea continues to prosper. Since the end of the Korean War, the Soviet Union has collapsed, but North Korea procured a nuclear capability despite U.S. presence on the peninsula. Regardless, three key facts emerge from U.S. presence in Korea. First, the ROK military is more capable and technologically advanced than their North Korean adversary despite the North's status as one of the largest militaries in the world. Second, fear of the spread of communism subsided in Northeast Asia when the Soviet Union collapsed and U.S.

---

[138] Suh Jae-Jung, "Allied to Race? The U.S.-Korea Alliance and Arms Race," *Asian Perspective* 33, no. 4 (2009): 113-16.

relations with China has since vastly improved. Lastly, the Republic of Korea has developed a much stronger economy and can afford the expenses of a superior military. Ironically, these are the same facts that influenced President Carter's wish to reduce U.S. military presence in Korea. The point, however, is clear. The U.S. military continues to maintain a robust force presence postured to fight against a conventional threat despite the heavy burden this commitment has placed on the U.S.

The strategic context for which U.S. forces are employed in Korea is defined by the operational environment, character of the threat, and character of friendly forces, while understanding it helps military leaders preserve vital national interests. Understanding the operational environment includes analysis of operational variables such as political, military, economic, and social circumstances. This monograph described these variables by outlining the history and background that set the foundation for U.S. policy and military presence in Korea. The separation of the two Koreas emerged as a byproduct of the end of World War II, while the threat of communist expansion by the Soviet Union set in motion U.S. policy that ensured the existence of free people and ideas around the world. North Korea strongly advocated communist principles and sought reunification with their southern neighbor when they started the Korean War. Although the North did not succeed, the resulting stalemate that has pervaded in Korea supports the DPRK's desire to focus economic output towards a strong military that can forcefully reunify the two countries. The ends, ways, and means of the threat and friendly forces define their character within the strategic context. While the South's focus has primarily been on building a strong conventional force, North Korea has since developed an asymmetric and nuclear capability to undermine the U.S./ROK alliance.

Although the strategic ends of the alliance to maintain stability between the two Koreas remains the same, the ways and means between the ROK and U.S. are seemingly different. The ROK aimed to defer costly military expenditures to their U.S. ally while they focused on their own economic growth and prosperity. For this, they have succeeded largely as they have grown into one of the largest economies in the world. Meanwhile, the U.S. continues to feel the effects of an economic crisis that has placed greater scrutiny on government expenditures. As a result, the Defense Department must reduce their budget by $487 billion over the next ten years. This will have great impacts on the way the U.S. military evolves, maintains, and deploys their force. It should also impact the ways and means for which it seeks stability in Korea.

This paper advocates changing the way the U.S. thinks about stability in Korea. Defining the operational environment throughout Korea's background and history, the character of the threat and friendly forces has changed in a manner that requires the U.S. to shift more of the security burden onto the ROK. Maintaining the status quo, as the U.S. has done, will incur more costs to American taxpayers even though the ROK economy can afford to fill the void departing U.S. forces will leave. In light of the strained U.S. economy and demand to reduce defense expenditures, military leaders must live up to their self-promoted mantra of innovative, agile, and adaptive leadership and incorporate the fundamentals of design to preserve vital national interests, including the economy. The United States and South Korea must seek to maintain their alliance, not a reliance.

APPENDIX

Mutual Defense Treaty between the Republic of Korea and the United States

Signed at Washington October 1, 1953
Entered into force November 17, 1954

The parties to this Treaty,

Reaffirming their desire to live in peace with all governments, and desiring to strengthen the fabric of Peace in the Pacific area.

Desiring to declare publicly and formally their common determination to defend themselves against external armed attack so that no potential aggressor could be under the illusion that either of them stand alone in the Pacific area.

Desiring further to strengthen their efforts for collective defense for the preservation of peace and security pending the development of a more comprehensive and effective system of regional security in the Pacific area.

Have agreed as follows:

Article 1

The Parties undertake to settle any international disputes in which they may be involved by peaceful means in such a manner that international peace and security and justice are not endangered and to refrain in their international relations from the threat or use of force in any manner inconsistent with the purposes of the United Nations, or obligations assumed by any Party toward the United Nations.

Article 2

The Parties will consult together whenever, in the opinion of either of them, the political independence or security of either of the Parties is threatened by external armed attack. Separately and jointly, by self-help and mutual aid, the Parties will maintain and develop appropriate means to deter armed attack and will take suitable measures in consultation and agreement to implement this Treaty and further its purposes.

Article 3

Each Party recognizes that an armed attack in the Pacific area on either of the Parties in territories now under their respective administrative control, or hereafter recognized by one of the Parties as lawfully brought under the administrative control of the other, would be dangerous to its own peace and safety and declares that it would act to meet the common danger in accordance with its constitutional processes.

Article 4

The Republic of Korea grants, and the United States of America accepts, the right to dispose United States land, air and sea forces in and about the territory of the Republic of Korea as determined by mutual agreement.

Article 5

This Treaty shall be ratified by the United States of America and the Republic of Korea in accordance with their respective constitutional processes and will come into force when instruments of ratification thereof have been exchanged by them at Washington.

Article 6

This Treaty shall remain in force indefinitely. Either party may terminate it in one year after notice has been given to the other Party.

IN WITNESS WHEREOF the undersigned plenipotentiaries have signed this Treaty.

DONE in duplicate at Washington, in the Korean and English languages, this first day of October 1953.

For the Republic of Korea:
/s/ Y.T. Pyun
For the United States of America:
/s/ John Foster Dulles

Understanding of the United States

It is the understanding of the United States that neither party is obligated, under Article III of the above Treaty, to come to the aid of the other except in case of an external armed attack against such party; nor shall anything in the present Treaty be construed as requiring the United States to give assistance to Korea except in the event of an armed attack against territory which has been recognized by the United States or lawfully brought under the administrative control of the Republic of Korea.

BIBLIOGRAPHY

Bajoria, Jayshree, and Youkyoung Lee. "The U.S.-South Korea Alliance." Council on Foreign Relations, http://www.cfr.org/south-korea/us-south-korea-alliance/p11459 (accessed October 28, 2011).

Bandow, Doug. "Why Are U.S. Troops Still in Korea?" *Forbes* (2011), http://www.forbes.com/sites/dougbandow/2011/05/03/why-u-s-troops-still-in-korea/ (accessed March 1, 2012).

Berry, William E., and Army War College (U.S.) Strategic Studies Institute. *The Invitation to Struggle: Executive and Legislative Competition over the U.S. Military Presence on the Korean Peninsula*. Carlisle Barracks, PA.: Strategic Studies Institute, U.S. Army War College, 1996.

Bowman, John S., ed. *Columbia Chronologies of Asian History and Culture*. New York: Columbia University Press, 2000.

Bureau of East Asian and Pacific Affairs, and U.S. Department of State. "South Korea." U.S. Department of State, http://www.state.gov/r/pa/ei/bgn/2800.htm (accessed October 28, 2011).

Buss, Claude Albert. *The United States and the Republic of Korea: Background for Policy*, Hoover International Studies. Stanford, Calif.: Hoover Institution Press, Stanford University, 1982.

Cato Institute. *Cato Handbook for Congress : 105th Congress*. Washington, DC: Cato Institute, 1997.

Cato Institute. Edward H. Crane, David Boaz, and ebrary Inc. "Cato Handbook for Congress: Policy Recommendations for the 108th Congress." Washington, DC: Cato Institute, 2003.

Cha, Victor D. "Hawk Engagement and Preventive Defense on the Korean Peninsula." *International Security* 27, no. 1 (2002): 40-78.

Chairman of the Joint Chiefs of Staff. *The National Military Strategy of the United States of America, 2011: Redefining America's Military Leadership*. Washington, DC: GPO, 2011.

Committee on Armed Services. *Hearing to Receive Testimony on U.S. Pacific Command and U.S. Forces Korea in Review of the Defense Authorization Request for Fiscal Year 2012 and the Future Years Defense Program*, April 12 2011.

Cordesman, Anthony H., and Andrew Gagel. *The Korean Military Balance: Comparative Korean Forces and the Forces of Key Neighboring States: Main Report*. Washington, DC: Center for Strategic and International Studies, 2011.

Council on Foreign Relations. Independent Task Force on U.S. Policy Toward the Korean Peninsula., Charles L. Pritchard, John H. Tilelli, Scott Snyder, and Richard Haass. *U.S. Policy toward the Korean Peninsula*. New York: Council on Foreign Relations, 2010.

Crawley, Vince. "General: Sweeten Tours in S. Korea." *Army Times* 62, no. 35 (2002): 12.

————. "Washington Eyes Ways to Sweeten S. Korea Tour." *Army Times* 64, no. 18 (2003): 16.

Cummings, John P. "Should the U.S. Continue to Maintain Forces in South Korea?". Carlisle Barracks, PA: U.S. Army War College, 2004.

Curtis, Gerald L., and Sung-ju Han. *The U.S.-South Korean Alliance: Evolving Patterns in Security Relations.* Lexington, Mass.: LexingtonBooks, 1983.

"Defense Management: Comprehensive Cost Information and Analysis of Alternatives Needed to Assess Military." *GAO Reports* (2011): 1.

Department of the Army. *FM 3-07.1: Security Force Assistance.* Washington, DC: GPO, 2009.

Department of the Army. *FM 5-0: The Operations Process.* Edited by Department of the Army. Washington, DC: GPO, 2010.

Department of Defense. "The 2008 National Defense Strategy." Washington, DC: U.S. GPO, 2008.

Department of Defense. "The 2010 Quadrennial Defense Review." Washington, DC: GPO, 2010.

Department of Defense. "Defense Budget Priorities and Choices." Washington, DC: GPO, 2012.

Department of Defense. "Sustaining U.S. Global Leadership: Priorities for 21st Century Defense." Washington, DC: GPO, 2012.

Dies Jr, Harry P. "North Korean Special Operations Forces: 1996 Kangnung Submarine Infiltration." *Military Intelligence Professional Bulletin* 30, no. 4 (2004): 29.

Dihora, Neal, and Rick Tauber. "Budget Control Act Bites into Defense." *Morningstar Stock Investor* 11, no. 3 (2011): 18-19.

"Economic Overview." In *United States Country Review*: CountryWatch Incorporated, 2010.

The Economist Pocket World in Figures, 2011 Edition. London, England: Penguin Group : Hamish Hamilton Ltd. in association with The Economist Newspaper Ltd., 2011.

Eirinberg, Keith, Scott Boller, and Georgetown University. Center for Strategic and International Studies. *Strengthening U.S.-Korean Relations in the Coming Years: A Report of the Csis U.S.-Korea Task Force*, Csis Panel Reports,. Washington, D.C.: Center for Strategic and International Studies, 1994.

Farrell Jr, Lawrence P. "Budget Control Act of 2011 Forces Real Cuts to Defense, and Difficult Choices." *National Defense* 96, no. 694 (2011): 4-4.

Freedman, Lawrence. *Deterrence.* Cambridge, UK ; Malden, MA: Polity Press, 2004.

Galbraith, James K. "On the Economics of Deficits." *American Prospect* 21, no. 9 (2010): A13-A15.

Garamone, Jim. "U.S.-Korean Defense Leaders Announce Exercise Invincible Spirit." *Armed Forces Press Service* (2010), http://www.defense.gov/news/newsarticle.aspx?id=60074 (accessed February 7, 2012).

Hanhimäki, Jussi M. *The Flawed Architect: Henry Kissinger and American Foreign Policy.* New York: Oxford University Press, 2004.

Harden, Blain. "North Korea Massively Increases Its Special Forces." *The Washington Post*, October 9, 2009. http://www.washingtonpost.com/wpdyn/content/article/2009/10/08/AR2009100804018.html (accessed March 1, 2012).

Harrison, Selig S. *Korean Endgame: A Strategy for Reunification and U.S. Disengagement.* Princeton, N.J.: Princeton University Press, 2002.

Harrison, Todd. "Analysis of the FY 2012 Defense Budget." Center for Strategic and Budgetary Assessments, 2011.

Harvie, Charles, Hy on-hun Yi, and Junggun Oh. *The Korean Economy: Post-Crisis Policies, Issues and Prospects.* Cheltenham, UK ; Northhampton, MA: Edward Elgar Pub., 2004.

Headquarters, Department of the Army. *ADP 3-0 Unified Land Operations.* Washington, DC: Department of the Army, 2011.

Howard, Michael, and Peter Paret. *Carl Von Clausewitz: On War.* Princeton, N.J.: Princeton University Press, 1984.

Howard, Peter. "Why Not Invade North Korea? Threats, Language Games, and U.S. Foreign Policy." *International Studies Quarterly* 48, no. 4 (2004): 805-28.

"Indefensible." *National Review* 64, no. 2 (2012): 16-16.

Jae-Jung, Suh. "Allied to Race? The U.S.-Korea Alliance and Arms Race." *Asian Perspective* 33, no. 4 (2009): 101-27.

Kim, Hyun-Dong. *Korea and the United States: The Evolving Transpacific Alliance in the 1960s,* Korean Unification Studies Series. Seoul, Korea: Research Center for Peace and Unification of Korea, 1990.

Kiseon, Chung, and Choe Hyun. "South Korean National Pride: Determinants, Changes, and Suggestions." *Asian Perspective* 32, no. 1 (2008): 99-127.

Kreisher, Otto. "Looming U.S. Defense Budget Cuts Could End a Decade of Jointness and a Growing Focus on Asia Could Mean Fewer U.S. Troops in Europe." *Naval Forces* 32, no. 6 (2011): 6-6.

Kwak, Tae-Hwan. *U.S.-Korean Relations, 1882-1982,* IFES Research Series. Seoul, Korea: Kyungnam University Press, 1982.

Kwak, Tae-Hwan, Wayne Pattersen, and Edward A. Olsen. *The Two Koreas in World Politics,* IFES Research Series. Seoul, Korea: Institute for Far Eastern Studies, Kyungnam University, 1983.

Ledford, Tranette. "Married to the Military -- and a Career, Too." *Army Times* 65, no. 30 (2005): 8.

Lee, Chae-Jin. *A Troubled Peace: U.S. Policy and the Two Koreas*. Baltimore: Johns Hopkins University Press, 2006.

Lee, Chung Min. "The Emerging Strategic Balance in Northeast Asia: Implications for Korea's Defense Strategy and Planning for the 1990's." PhD, Published for the Research Center for Peace and Unification of Korea by Seoul Computer Press, Fletcher School of Law and Diplomacy, Tufts University, 1989.

Levin, Carl (U.S. Senator). "Floor Statement on the National Defense Authorization Act for Fiscal Year 2012." 2011.

———. "Hearing to Receive Testimony on U.S. Pacific Command and U.S. Forces Korea in Review of the Defense Authorization Request for Fiscal Year 2012 and the Future Years Defense Program." (2011).

———. "Senate Armed Services Committee Completes Conference of National Defense Authorization Act for Fiscal Year 2012." 2011.

Levin, Norman D. *Do the Ties Still Bind?: The U.S.-ROK Security Relationship after 9/11*. Santa Monica, CA: Rand Corporation, 2004.

Manyin, Mark E., Emma Chantell-Avery, Mary Beth Nikitin, and Library of Congress: Congressional Research Service. *U.S.-South Korea Relations: CRS Report for Congress*. Washington, D.C.: Congressional Research Service, Library of Congress, 2011.

Marshment, Kelvin C. "The U.S. Ground Combat Experience in Korea: In Defense of U.S. Interests or a Strategic Dinosaur." Command and General Staff College, 1983.

McDougall, Walter A. *Promised Land, Crusader State: The American Encounter with the World since 1776*. Boston: Houghton Mifflin, 1997.

Meiertöns, Heiko. *The Doctrines of Us Security Policy: An Evaluation under International Law*. Cambridge: Cambridge University Press, 2010.

The Military Balance, 2011. IISS Publication. London,: International Institute for Strategic Studies.

Millett, Allan Reed. *The War for Korea, 1950-1951: They Came from the North*, Modern War Studies. Lawrence: University Press of Kansas, 2010.

"North Korean Special Forces." In *IHS Jane's: Defence & Security Intelligence & Analysis*: IHS Global Limited, 2011.

Obama, Barack. "Address before a Joint Session of the Congress on the State of the Union." 1: Superintendent of Documents, 2011.

Oberdorfer, Don. *The Two Koreas: A Contemporary History*. New ed. New York: Basic Books, 2001.

Ohn, Chang-Il. "The Joint Chiefs of Staff and U.S. Policy and Strategy Regarding Korea, 1945-1953." University of Kansas, 1983.

Olsen, Edward A. *U.S. Policy and the Two Koreas*. San Francisco: World Affairs Council of Northern California, 1988.

Patel, Nirav, and Lindsey Ford. "The Future of the U.S.-Rok Alliance: Global Perspectives." *Korean Journal of Defense Analysis* 21, no. 4 (2009): 401-16.

Pauly, Robert J. *The Ashgate Research Companion to Us Foreign Policy*. Farnham, England ; Burlington, Vt.: Ashgate, 2010.

Peloso, Jennifer. *The Two Koreas*, The Reference Shelf. New York: H.W. Wilson, 2004.

Pritchard, Charles L. *Failed Diplomacy: The Tragic Story of How North Korea Got the Bomb*. Washington, D.C.: Brookings Institution Press, 2007.

Rapp-Hooper, Mira, and Kenneth N. Waltz. "What Kim Jong-Il Learned from Qaddafi's Fall: Never Disarm." *The Atlantic* (2011).

Rep. Howard P. Buck Mckeon, R. Calif Chairman. "Representative Howard P. Buck Mckeon, R-Calif., Holds a Hearing on the Budget for the U.S. Pacific Command and U.S. Forces Korea." 2011.

Samuelson, Robert J. "Rethinking the Great Recession." *Wilson Quarterly* 35, no. 1 (2011): 16.

Scalapino, Robert A., and Hongkoo Lee. *Korea-U.S. Relations: The Politics of Trade and Security*, Research Papers and Policy Studies. Berkeley: Institute of East Asian Studies, University of California, 1988.

Schnabel, James F. *Policy and Direction: The First Year*, United States Army in the Korean War, V. 3. Washington, D.C.: Office of the Chief of Military History, United States Army, 1972.

Scully, Megan. "Proposed Defense Budget Cuts Draw Battle Lines within Gop." *Sea Power* 54, no. 3 (2011): 6.

Sharp, Walter L. "Statement of General Walter L. Sharp Commander, United Nations Command; Commander, United States-Republic of Korea Combined Forces Command; and Commander, United States Forces Korea before the House Armed Services Committee, April 6, 2011."

Stanton, Joshua. "It's Time for the U.S. Army to Leave Korea." *CBS News* (2010), http://www.cbsnews.com/2100-215_162-6386737.html (accessed March 1, 2012).

Truman, Harry S. "Recommendation for Assistance to Greece and Turkey: Address of the President of the United States." edited by U.S. House of Representatives. Washington, D.C., 1947.

United States of America, 112th Congress. "National Defense Authorization Act for Fiscal Year 2012." edited by U.S. Congress. Washington, DC: U.S. Congress, 2012.

United States and Republic of Korea. *Mutual Defense Treaty between the United States of America and the Republic of Korea, Signed at Washington October 1, 1953*. Washington, D.C.: U.S. Govt. Print. Off., 1953.

"United States Forces Korea." USFK Public Affairs, http://www.usfk.mil/usfk/ (accessed December 10, 2011).

U.S. Congress. Senate. *Budget Control Act of 2011*. Washington, DC: GPO, 2011.

University of Southern California. Korean Studies Institute., and Korea Economic Institute (U.S.). *Towards Sustainable Economic & Security Relations in East Asia: U.S. and ROK Policy Options*, Joint U.S.-Korea Academic Studies. Washington, D.C.: Korea Economic Institute, 2008.

Van Der Putten, Frans-Paul. "The Sustainability of the US Military Presence in East Asia." *Studia Diplomatica* 64, no. 3 (2011): 67-78.

Wensinger, Jeremy. "Supporting the Warfighter: Adapting to the Changing Paradigm of the Defense Market." *Microwave Journal* 53, no. 1 (2010): 24-38.

The White House. "The 2010 National Security Strategy." Washington, DC: GPO, 2010.

White House Office of the Press Secretary. "Joint Vision for the Alliance of the United States of America and the Republlic of Korea." edited by The White House. Washington, DC: Office of the Press Secretary, 2009.

Wolf Jr, Charles. "Korean Reunification: How It Might Come About and at What Cost." *Defence & Peace Economics* 17, no. 6 (2006): 681-90.